THE PHILLIP KEVEREN SERIES — BIG NOTE PIANO

THE NUTCRACKER

CONTENTS

— PIANO LEVEL —
LATE ELEMENTARY/EARLY INTERMEDIATE
(HLSPL LEVEL 3-4)

ISBN 978-0-634-04866-1

Visit Hal Leonard Online at
www.halleonard.com

World headquarters, contact:
Hal Leonard
7777 West Bluemound Road
Milwaukee, WI 53213
Email: info@halleonard.com

In Europe, contact:
Hal Leonard Europe Limited
1 Red Place
London, W1K 6PL
Email: info@halleonardeurope.com

In Australia, contact:
Hal Leonard Australia Pty. Ltd.
4 Lentara Court
Cheltenham, Victoria, 3192 Australia
Email: info@halleonard.com.au

OVERTURE

Pyotr Il'yich Tchaikovsky
Arranged by Phillip Keveren

Allegro (𝅗𝅥 = 96)

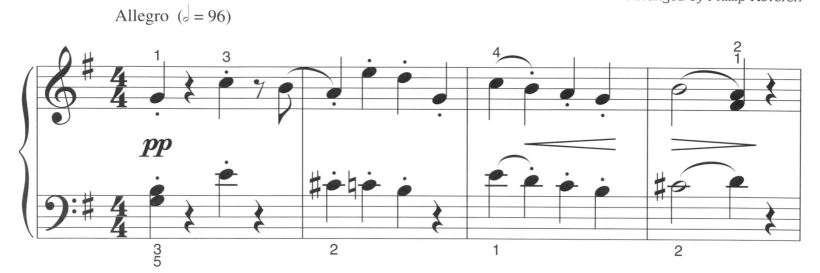

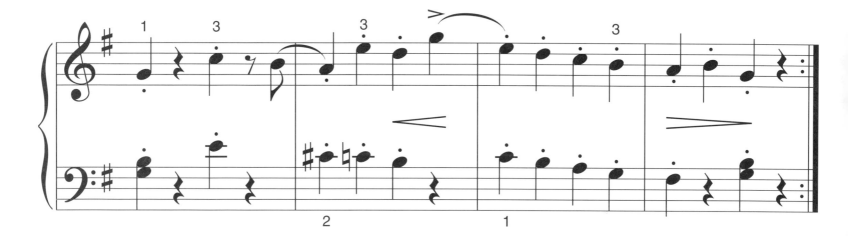

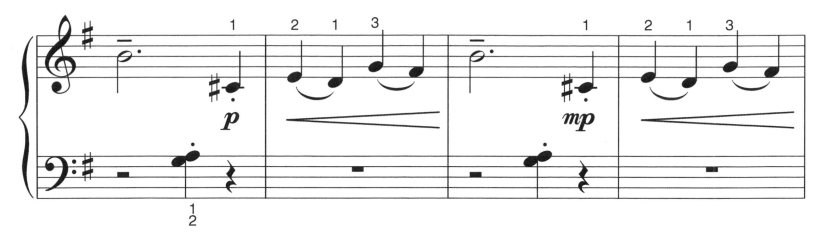

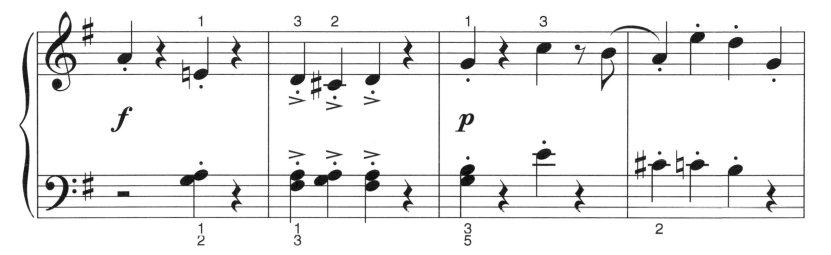

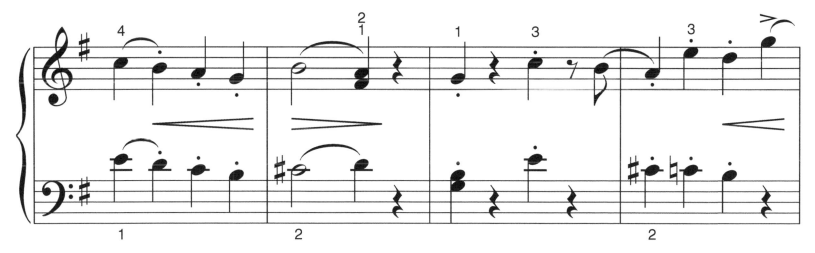

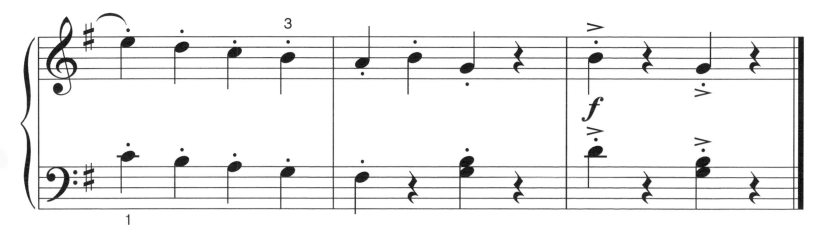

MARCH

Pyotr Il'yich Tchaikovsky
Arranged by Phillip Keveren

Tempo di Marcia (♩ = 120)

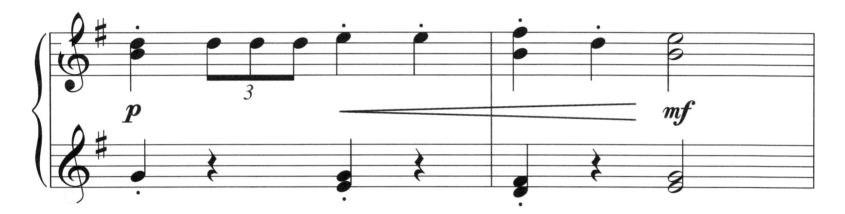

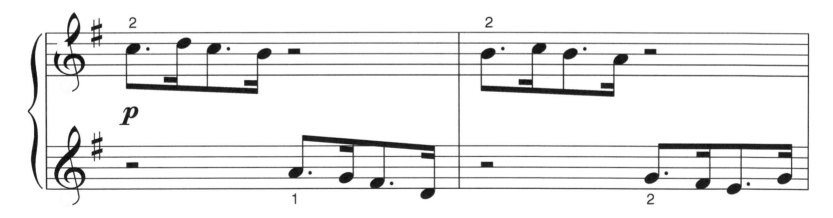

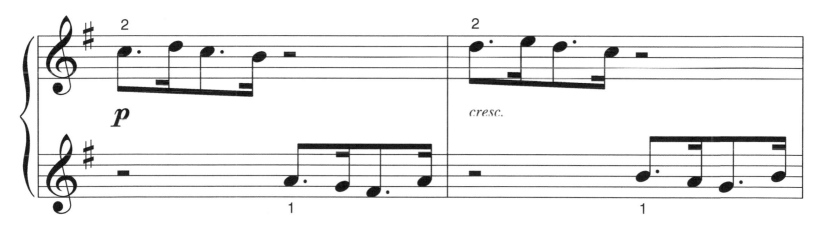

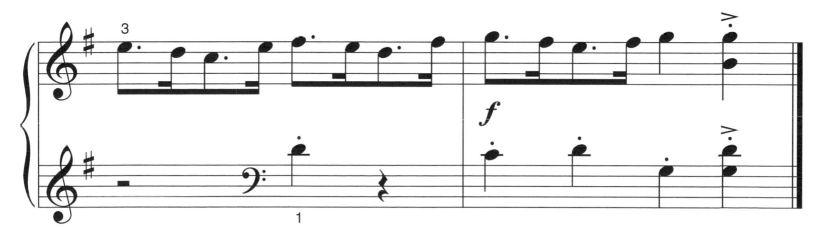

DANCE OF THE SUGAR PLUM FAIRY

Pyotr Il'yich Tchaikovsky
Arranged by Phillip Keveren

Andante (♩ = 112)

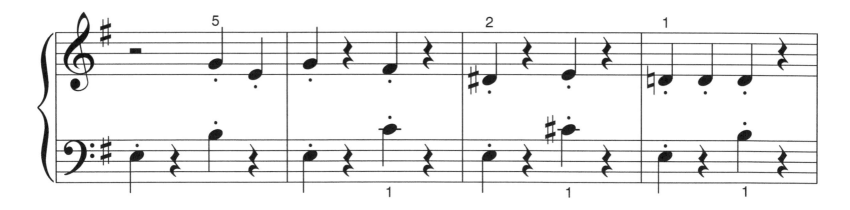

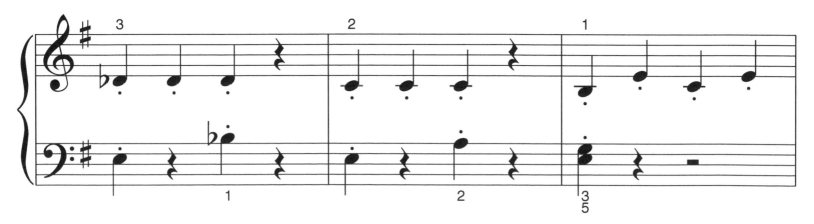

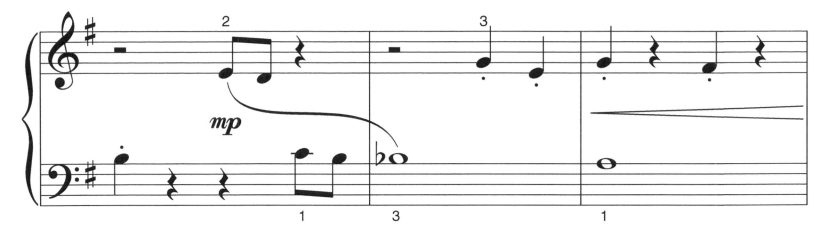

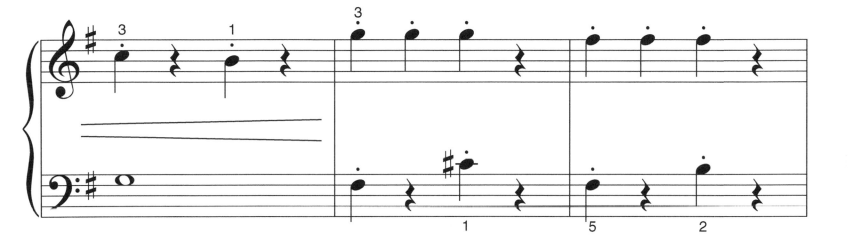

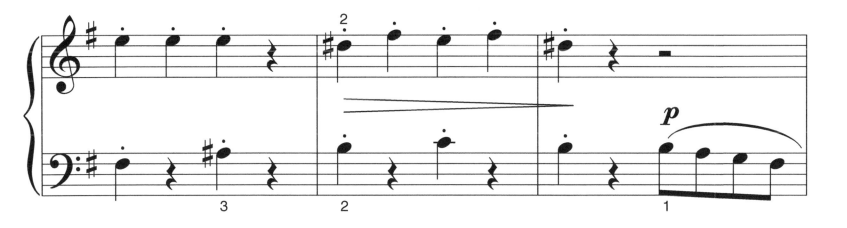

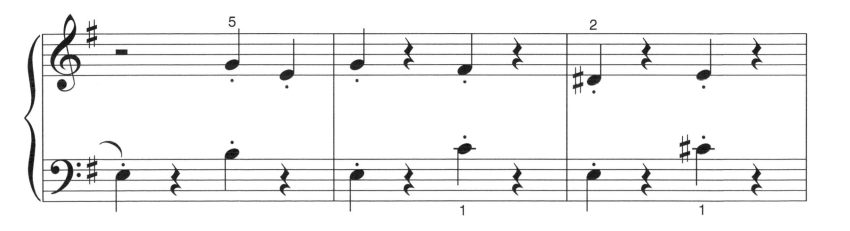

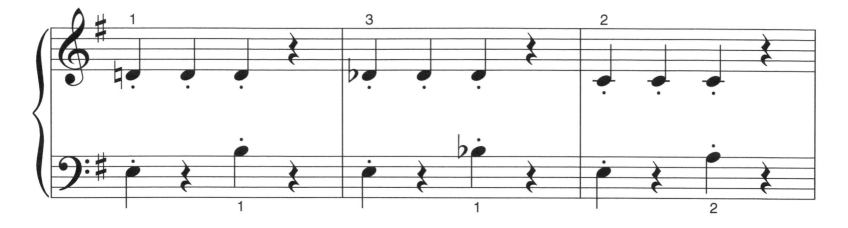

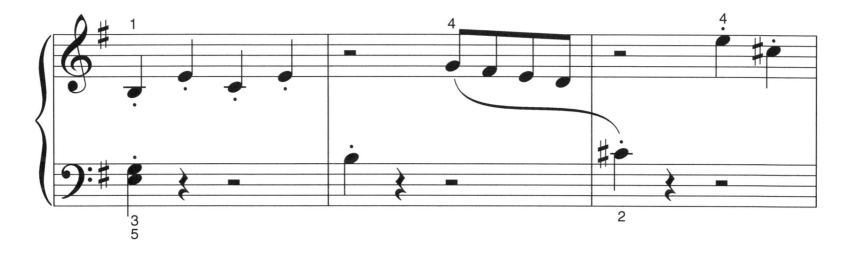

RUSSIAN DANCE
(Trépak)

Pyotr Il'yich Tchaikovsky
Arranged by Phillip Keveren

Vivace (♩ = 126)

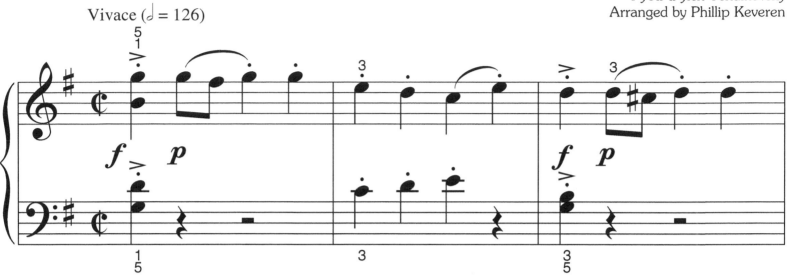

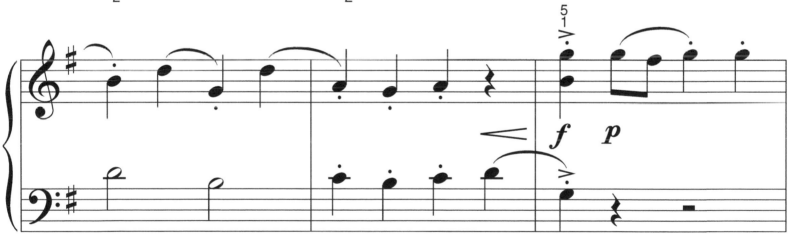

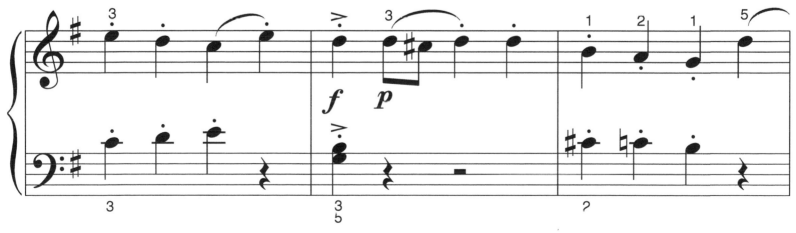

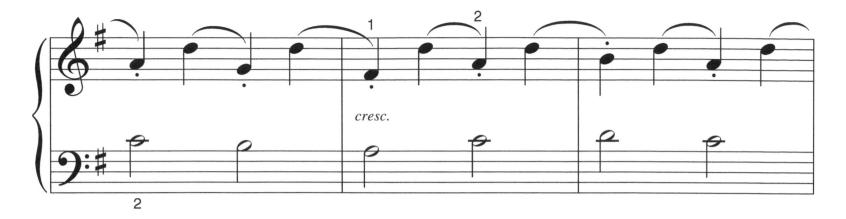

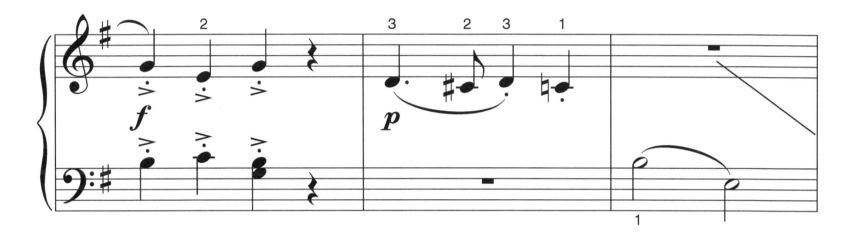

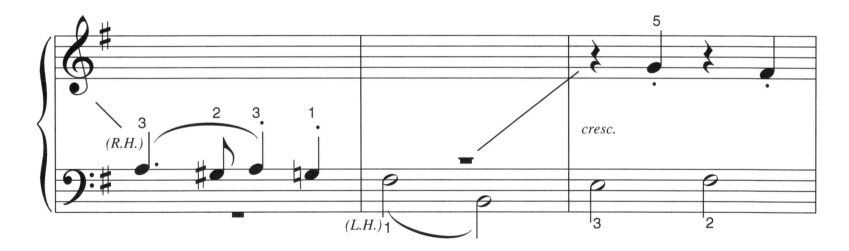

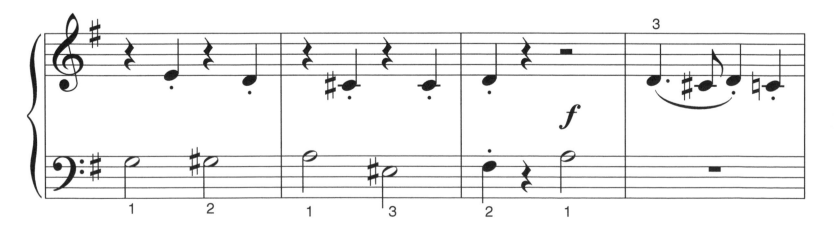

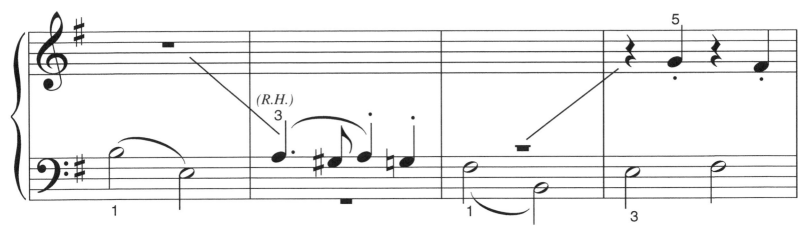

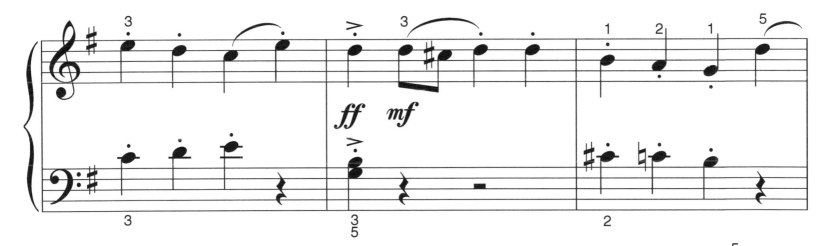

ARABIAN DANCE

Pyotr Il'yich Tchaikovsky
Arranged by Phillip Keveren

Allegretto (♩ = 138)

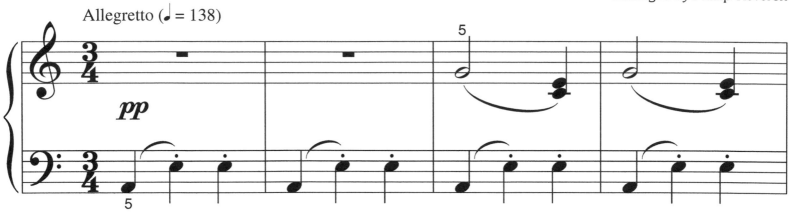

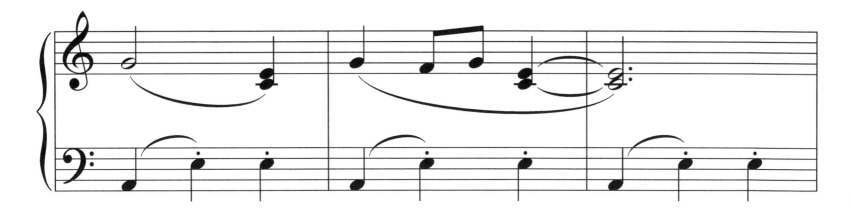

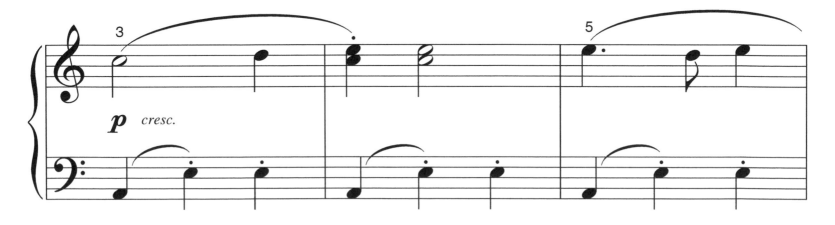

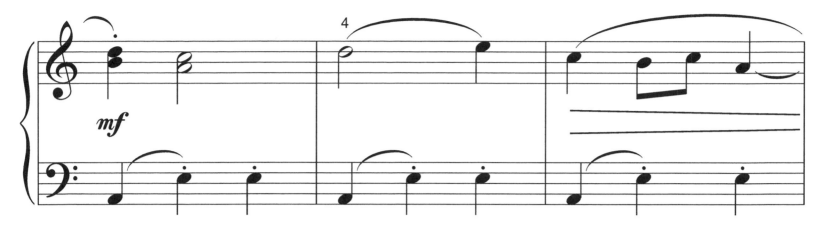

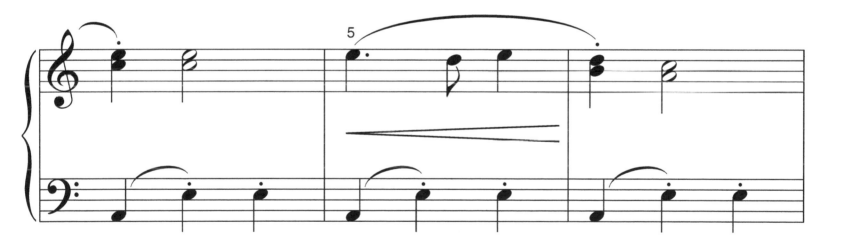

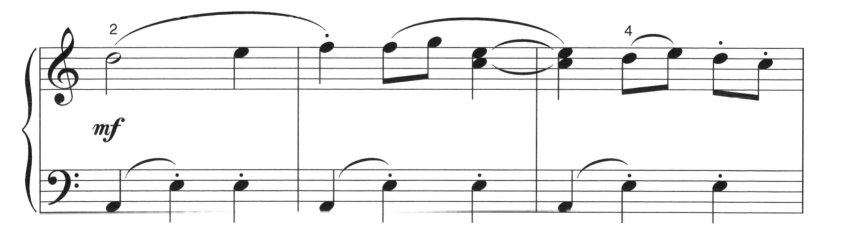

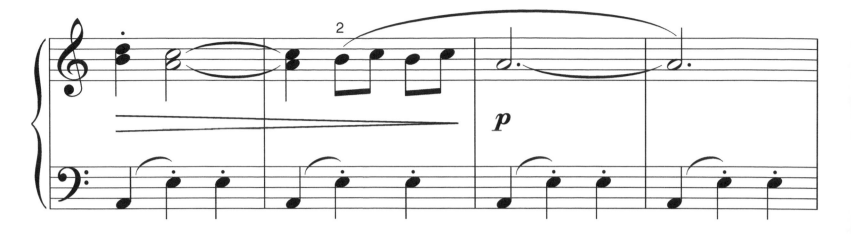

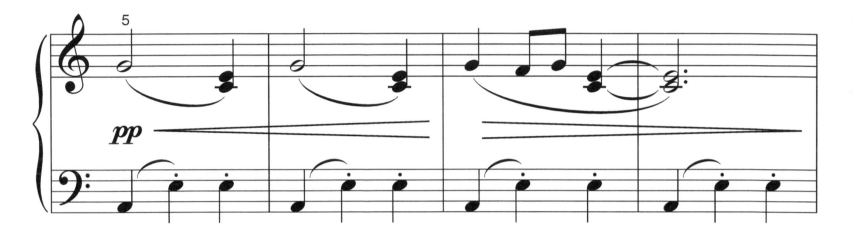

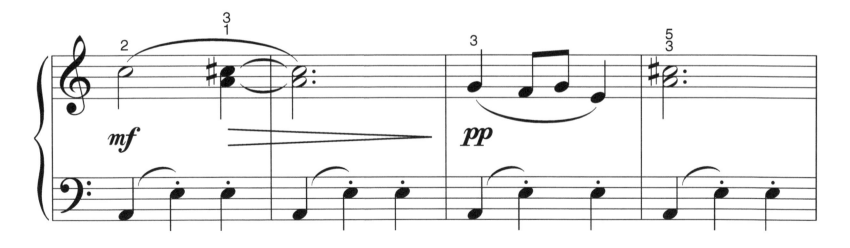

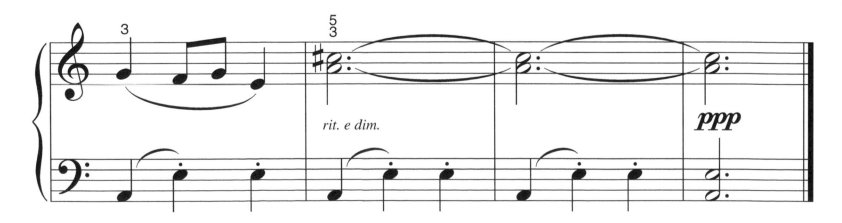

CHINESE DANCE

Pyotr Il'yich Tchaikovsky
Arranged by Phillip Keveren

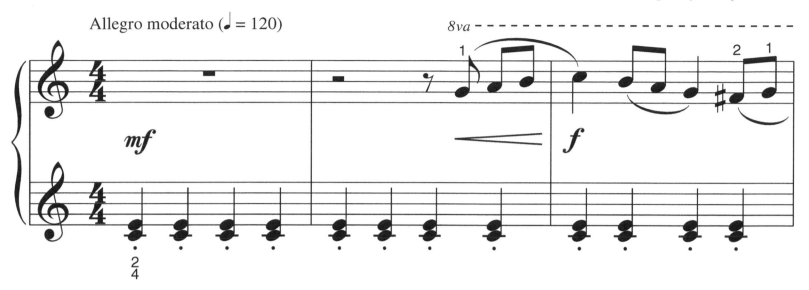

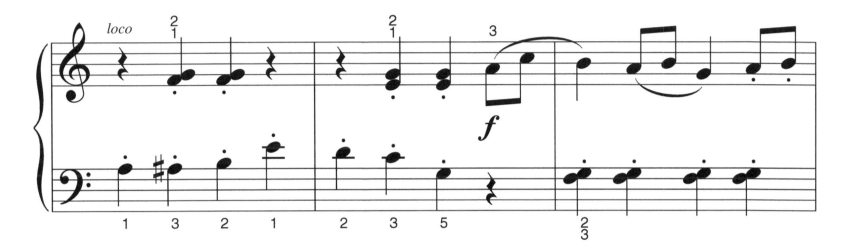

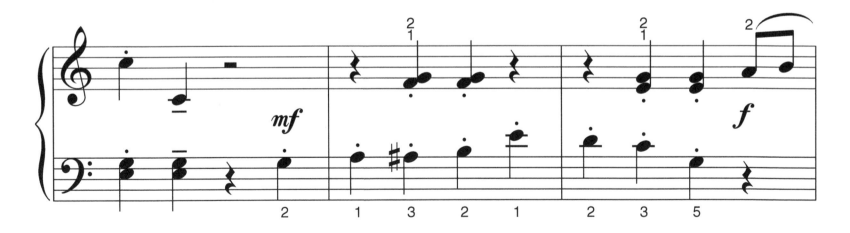

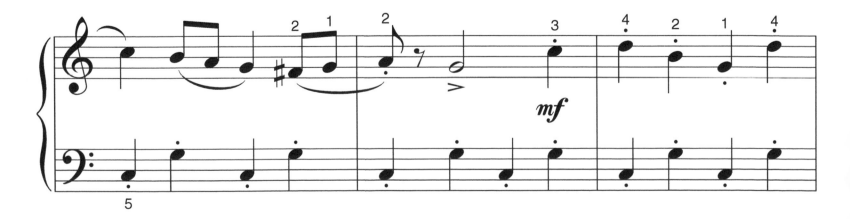

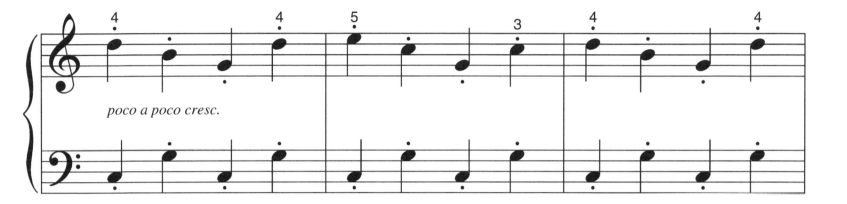

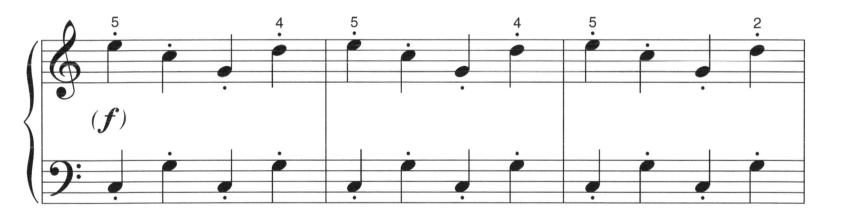

WALTZ OF THE FLOWERS

Pyotr Il'yich Tchaikovsky
Arranged by Phillip Keveren

Tempo di Valse (♩. = 52)

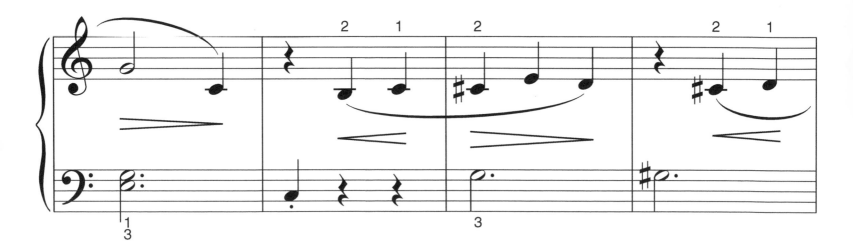

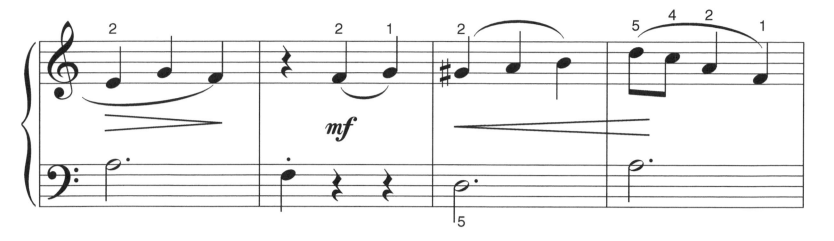

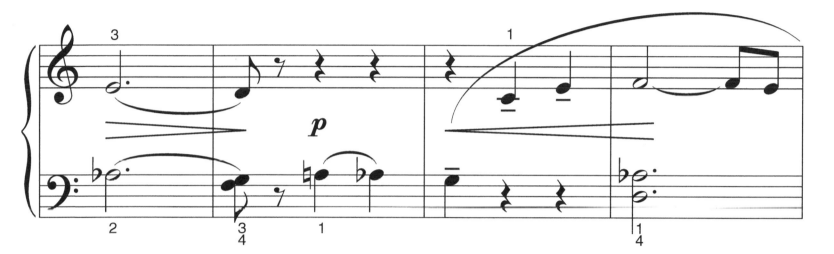

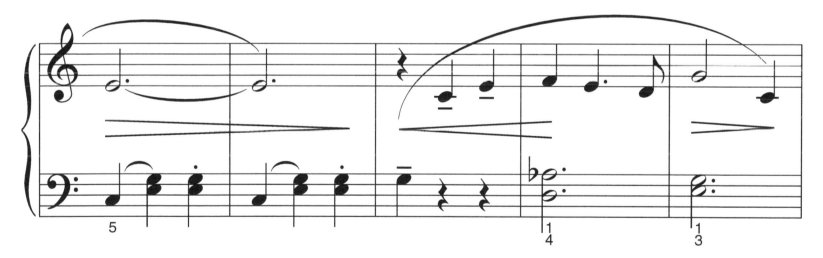

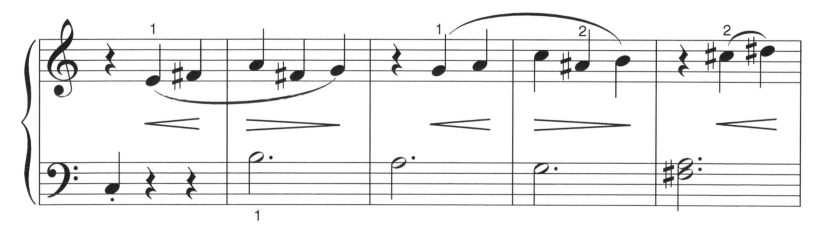

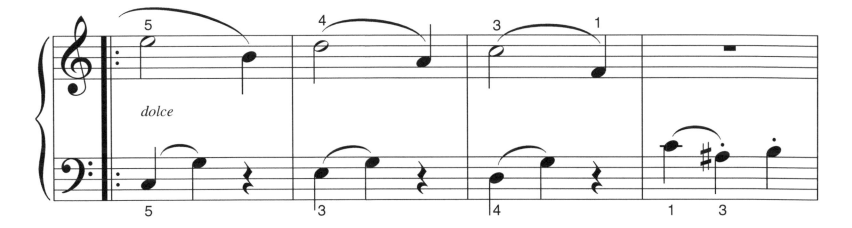

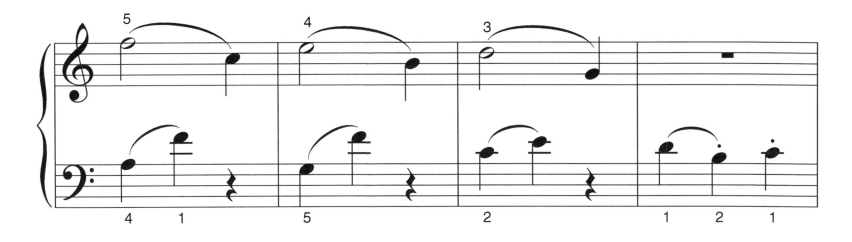

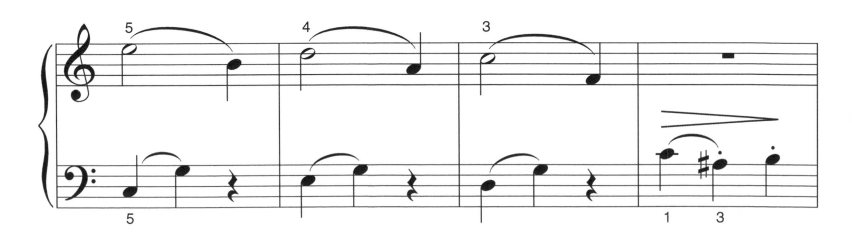

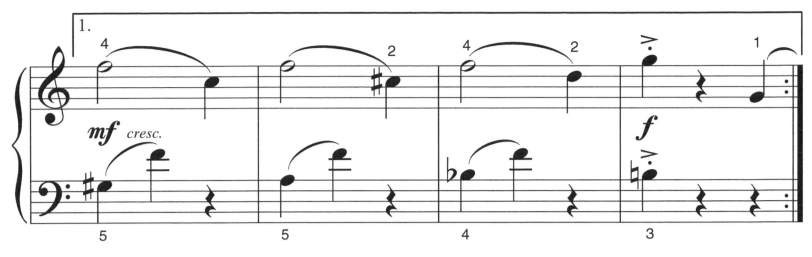

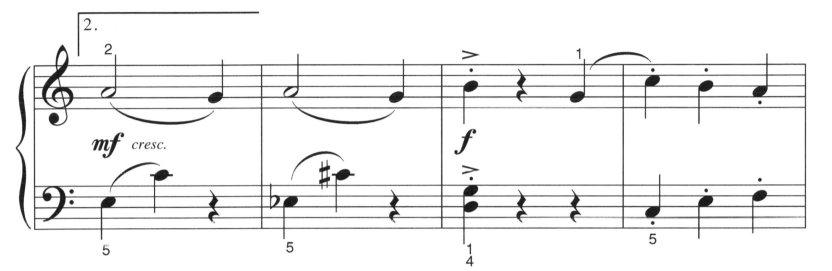

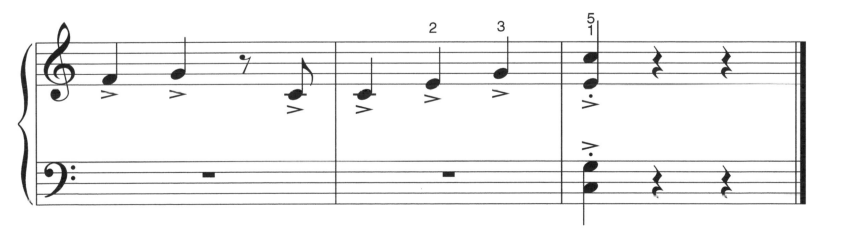

DANCE OF THE REED-FLUTES

Pyotr Il'yich Tchaikovsky
Arranged by Phillip Keveren

Andantino (♩ = 128)

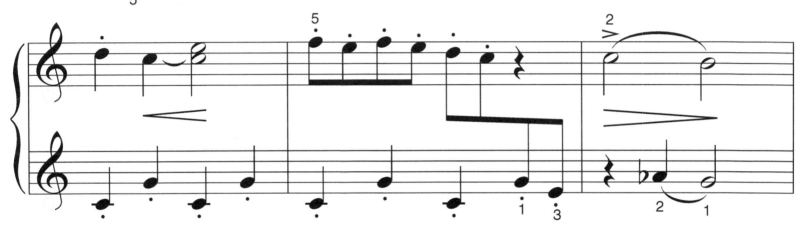

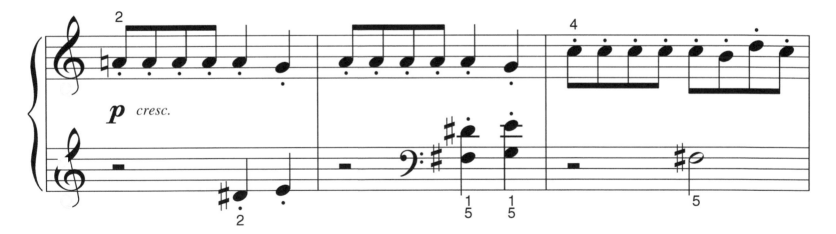

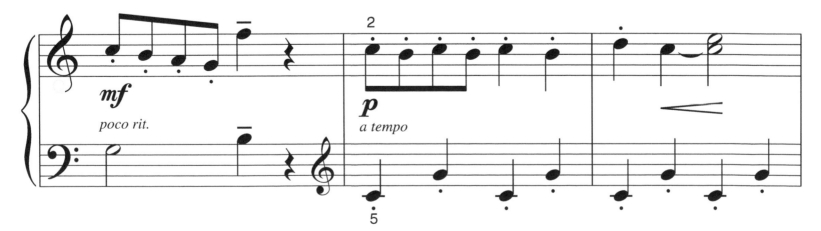

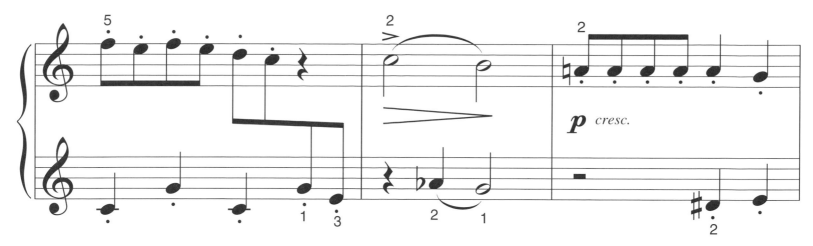

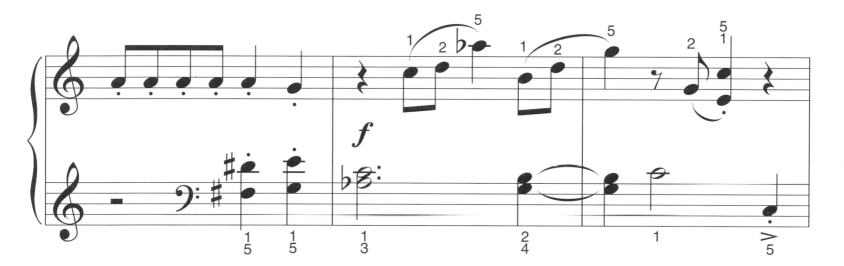

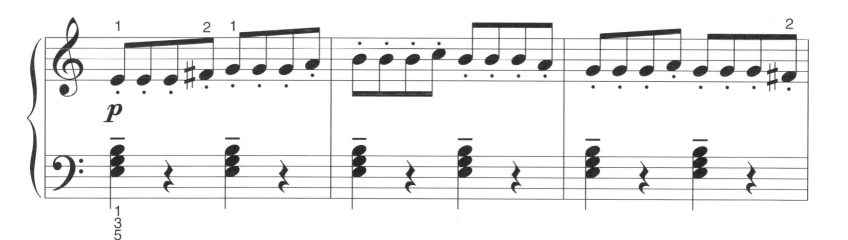

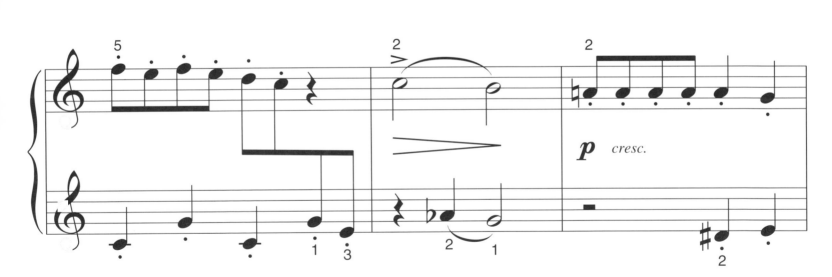

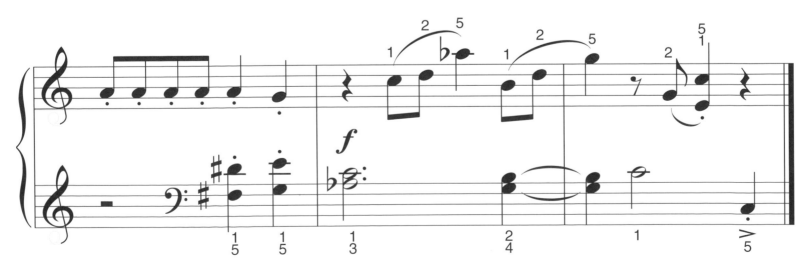